The
HUNGERING
SOUL
EMERGES

A Book of Poetry

BY RISHI JAISWAL

GRATITUDE

❧

I would like to dedicate to this book to my loving siblings:
Raj and Reeti Jaiswal who have always been there for me
through the ups and downs. My pillars of strength.
Thanks for everything
and I promise we will always stick together no matter what.

and thank you:
Bittu Bhai (Mayank Jaiswal)
My mother Deepa Jaiswal
Natasha Aggarwal
Natasha Sayani
Nitesh Pymagam
Rohan Desai

wouldn't be here without any of you

and last but not least
thank you for opening my book:
I sincerely hope it touches and inspires you in some way

TABLE OF CONTENTS

"What has the past told us? What have we learned

from it and what have we ignored?"

RISHI JAISWAL

WAITING FOR TOMORROW

Beads of sweat form above a frowning brow,

A frustrating silence where no music is allowed,

Fear has its own rhythm to which I rock back and forth,

Swaying in sweet agony searching for a dream to abort,

The stairwell seems too dark and the ladder's a bit slippery,

The clouds have all dried up and the mountainside's just too steep,

A misery overshadowing those searching for peace and nobility,

A river abandoning thirst is a journey that embraces tragedy,

So I wait admiring this Great Wall I built brick by brick,

Carefully cemented, juxtaposed are my worries, fears and guilt,

A shrine in front of which I can now rightfully bow down,

I simply read my prayers aloud, smiling, awaiting my crown,

Dream infinity I can and talk of things grand,

Situating myself comfortably in the shoes of a man,

But when responsibility dawns truth, through the cracks in my wall,

Will those words manifest royalty or on my knees will I crawl?

Have faith and confidence become my weapons against reality?

Torturing hope amounting to pure, worthless anxiety,

Or will this flame of passion choose to feed me over burning me alive,

Because if my dream burns then so do I,

So til its salvation, my completion, I must and will survive,

And believe beyond patient waiting a new horizon resides,

I will try! I will try! I will try! I will try!

Overstepping some of the more weaker and subtler why's,

"Almost there!" screams chest, reaching, reminding me of Will defined:

"It is your vision's strength, its ability," it says, " to make your reality lie.

"To make mountaintops crumble and make planets align,

"So dip your brush in true soul, paint your voice across skies,

"Quit the eternal wait for tomorrow or watch your dreams dry"

TAKE A SECOND

I remember back when times were tough and lonely,

The world seemed too big, too fast, too phony,

Women seemed like a mystery

Happiness seemed like cold history,

The same question tearing my mind to shreds,

Is this me? Or is this more me eating me, by insecurity?

Kick a rhyme alone once in a while to vibe,

Only time I let the pain out from behind my eyes,

Had to do what I could to keep that temporary smile alive,

And that? Well, that was just elementary school guys!

Ahead to come was chasing life's high after high,

In the pursuit of a why, or what's the point,

Or a might as well die,

And revive as an angel with a real ability to save lives,

Not just in theory, in retrospect, or on a piece of paper,

Or hiding in the head of some brilliant moviemaker,

Not just to those who can reach out to you,

But to those who are god's forgotten few,

The kids who don't deserve the crooked hand their dealt,

Extensions of their parents' misfortune or lack of wealth,

Or of even varying degrees of psychological health,

The kids who live as victims from their cradle to their grave,

Or the kids who feel they need to victimize,

So they themselves can feel safe,

Cut the roots of the issue and burn it all down,

No more irreparable damage to young minds in town,

A future now of unbounded possibilities,

A potential unlocked is what I want to see,

A middle finger now to the status quo,

Say, "This has been my world now, since I was one day old!"

"Truth be told and re-told:

What is life without Love?"

WHAT TO CALL THIS

I don't know what to call this push,

Chasing you as though something precious you took,

Thinking about your voice to fall asleep,

And through my dreams hear your sweet melody,

Wake up holding on- to what's long been gone,

Hoping, just one more minute in dreamland might right my wrongs,

An imprint that you had left on my heart long ago,

Inscribed with ink, a lingering touch that just won't go,

A compelling power you still seem to have over me,

Running away from you means standing illusions curtaining reality.

Maybe a lie was told when I said this was a possibility?

Or is it the manifestation of guilt for once pushing you off that tree?

When you left I told everyone, I said, "I have shelved her love."

Not burnt entirely. Just something I shouldn't be thinking of.

My high school sweetheart you would always be,

Even if it meant you were happier without me,

Told our stories and kept you, for years, alive within,

Hoping by some miracle in my life, not dreams, you would reappear,

And here you are a beautiful illusion of mist,

An imaginative unreality of empty lips,

A tease, someone brick-walled the door to my bliss,

A raft with holes, a true hit and miss,

A few lines that surface a tragedy,

A mirror showing how much you mean to me,

And at its core, simple irony,

In the fact that after all this, we can't be,

So I'll let the pen spill heart and the ink my blues,

On the way dropping a few transparent clues:

A man with a huge heart and understandably a few issues,

But will keep you happy eternally for his every word to you is true,

I will hold and love you for always if that is what you ever choose,

And its reasoning lies in simplicity:

My day begins and ends with you.

"What is it we are constantly searching for?

Why are we here?

What is this anxious curiosity?"

BEYOND THE LOST

What do we want?

We want time…

Time away from people, but with them too,

We want time to roam the world,

But also time to get to know our immediate surroundings better.

We want to plan every moment perfectly so we can breathe in the moment,

We want time to figure out what everything means within a textbook outside:

The real,

We want to scream silently and protest against ourselves.

A bit much?

That's why we want it! An eccentric desire to conquer all,

The real all, the inner-, the outer-, while staying at peace with ourselves, our friends and everything else, for that matter.

We want to make people feel better but not at the expense of our own free will and feelings…But then we kinda do?

This I here wants to hypnotize people,

Into believing that we are indeed from the same planet and that us being able to understand each other, the fact that we look alike, might actually be more than a mere coincidence, and it might just mean that

we are on the same

Goddamned team. Maybe?

Team Humanity! So we should stop killing each other, maybe?

Just in case we might need each other one day,

When a true threat presents itself,

Not those we make up only for the stubborn purpose,

Of separating ourselves from others. Why do we bother?

We are all here as unique individuals as is right?

So then what is this want?

We want to be gods!

By knowing god as the soul connecting us to everything that exists,

The us: the we, far more than just the I's we must create to survive;

From that which begins from within us…and branches out to all

others.

To every bit of creation that surrounds our being.

Finally being immersed in the beauty of this world

And truly becoming one with it…

And thus of it.

Complexity reduced to this simplicity that we just want more!

Call it growth, call it ambition, or call it fodder for the soul,

Please feed the us beyond the lost I, for our soul is hungry!

Isn't yours?

WHERE DO I BELONG?

Where do I belong?

What is my purpose?

Why was I thrown down here?

Why do such questions sometimes make life feel so worthless?

Who can talk to me now? Who can whisper this in my ear?

Who can point me down a path, which will make this clearer?

No matter where I go I seem to fit in no socket,

I dig deep in my soul for an answer, like for change in a pocket,

Why do I tremble with doubt, every single step I take?

Why does this insecurity broaden as though my life were at stake?

I'm being tossed back and forth and with great pain. Bidding adieu,

Life just passes me by with time; I follow without a clue,

I'm looking for that spot where the sun hits just right.

No more can I roam in darkness I want to kiss the sky, a kite,

Shrouded in mist, blind, reaching out for a hand:

Someone to grab me and pull me in and say, "This is your home land,

"This is where you belong–with us till the end,

"Where you don't have to fight yourself every moment,

"But live free smiling, breathing without repent."

Somebody to guide me away from pain me with your love.

Show me a new reality instead of soaring, deluded, far above,

Curtain me from pain and confusion and hatred above all.

Let me find myself through you,

Your eyes must help me to one–day stand tall,

"Where are you?!" I call left standing, waiting–

Debating rest at the station or upon the good tracks…

"Failure is a Gift in Disguise.
The Only Real Teacher in Life."

RESPONSE

❧

When a lifestyle turns to a memory,
And catastrophe hits where you fail to see,
When you strive through your life to plant a seed,
Only to realize it grew into the wrong type of tree,
When only drugs or liquor can cover misery,
When you can't stop pain for inside is where you bleed,
When you know you slipped up and to the sky you plead,
Wondering what went wrong. Was it the love? Or it's greed?
When tears come down and freeze on your cheek,
Because of the cold you feel inside so deep,

Can I take control of time and rewind it back?
Before I hurt someone I love, I'd rather raise the gat,
Feel the cold nozzle up against my temple,
Realizing life's dimensions, it just can't be that simple.
By ending this gift not a single problem solved,
Then I am no man, just another lost cause.
People say if you slip you can get back up,
I fell in quick sand with shattered kneecaps.
I'm weak now from being poked and stabbed in the chest,
As my heart failed, gave up, so did the rest.
I sank giving up in weakness up to my neck,
Thinking somehow I need to cheat life, cheat pain, cheat death.
I shiver as I clench every joint, every single muscle flexed,
And rise above all in the breath versus worth test.

I see clearly one thing and one thing alone,
You gotta' fight now till the end, gotta' grind your bones.
You can't fix these problems: all you can do in the end is learn,
Come out stronger, smarter, tougher, more experienced and stern,

You would think that I'd say, "Replant the seed."
Not a chance! Bend the roots of that tree to fulfill what you need,
Wake up, get out, go grab what you want.
Don't succumb to this life's cruel and painful taunts.

Know what ever happens that you control it.
You rise, you're god, step the hell up and own it.
Next time be careful when you walk into a fog,
When you're half way in don't go complaining to mom.
You made this decision; it was all your choice.
Own up, be smart, don't whine and keep making noise,

Sweat is diamond and blood can be wiped,
You'll be paid in full if you do things right,
Grab the opportunity when only you see it fit,
No guiding lights here, only your mind that is lit,

I want what I need, but I know I have to put in the work,
Long times have passed, but situations must rebirth,
I'm going to make it happen now, plant my feet in this earth,
Do it over again if I have to, watch me shatter this curse,
I never chose this life; it was life that chose me,
But today I chose you life,
To push me beyond fragile eternity.

"It's how we choose to see the world around us that shapes our experience here"

JUXTAPOSE, SUPERIMPOSE PERCEPTION: THE EXPLORATION

In a dome I'm trapped topping one hundred degrees,

I see my brown skin melt and fall like autumn leaves off trees,

I wait for this mask to melt so I may once again breathe with ease,

The darker the night, the darker the nightmares swallow peace dreams,

What am I but flesh and bone? What is an average to this world?

What difference would it make if I vanished into the red eye of the devil?

What would it matter if I took one hundred thousand people?

Purpose. Define it for yourself and no one else.

Now look into the mirror that is that very definition:

Purpose. A fetus, to an infant, to a toddler, to a kid, to a teen, to an adult, to middle age, to ice age, to death.

There is no balance between good and evil.

Good and Evil are results of varying magnifying glass angles with which we view the world around us.

A Ghost Town is where I want to be,

As I can affect no other, with a single wrong deed.

Roaming in black, the unknown is a mystery;

No boundaries, nor for lines is there need.

Float away or float back, float free, float trapped, swim there where

you most expect to be zapped,

Lost I will be until I find my walking stick,

Lost I will stay without finding the light you lit,

Taking the first steps in nothingness where everything created is

perfection,

The head bows down equally here, to every idea, suggestion, feeling,

and illusion,

Nothing is perfect, as perfect is nothingness,

As life overflows you usurp it,

Torn between heaven and hell, the non-existent realms pull me

towards them,

I want demarcations and lines to define what I do.

But who will tell me to feel at peace with my decisions or

uncomfortable,

I will.

But what if I want to change those demarcations to fit my life and to

be MORE at peace with a larger percent of things I'm doing.

Where does that leave me?

Am I then truly at peace?

Am I god then? For I define right or wrong.

Or in that case am I Satan?

Either way I wield an arm of good or evil.

I have two hands hence I wield arms of both, one of each hand.

Sandy Beaches you are just as confused as I am,

Are you water of the ocean or of earth you are sand?

I robot, metal replaced by bone marrow, tissue and heart,

My heart is a drum, pumps red blood, but love it does not,

I need to wear a mask to tell my CPU that I am not a robot on this

planet,

I, for one, have no purpose for any being, so my one hundred years here

is not written or planned yet,

Oh shadows you intrigue me with your ways,

Figures floating around yet devoid of their names,

The figures can do as they please and cross the lines they have set for themselves of wrong and right,

Since they are no more John, Rishi, or Michael, but a momentary

imprint crystallized,

Even our empty counterparts are fully realized

Shadows blanket all. We are all each other.

Under her arm we are all the same.

Who am I? Who cares!

I am black, like the more demonic nights.

You, oh shadows, can rid the world of several by reaching your

Ever extending arms out into the light and chomping it away

Like it never existed.

No need to pretend, no need to wear a mask, to hide your inability to

define everything around you so you are at a comfort level that is

higher than those around you to make yourself feel important.

To make you feel like you are worth more than the air you breathe.

To prove to yourself more than anything;

That you are more than a mere volume occupier,

To not blend into the tie-dye of confused emotions this world is,

To say that,"A Shadow cannot devour me!"

A smile is a frown upside down right?

Then turn me the right side up with all your might.

Gravity tells us what is up and what's down,

What does it matter though? For underwater either way you drown,

Perception.

A world filled with volume occupiers. We are here to set a balance of

something that we are unaware of.

You are an individual. Or not. You disappear and you will be replaced

by tears captured in handkerchiefs, which will

Be thrown away sooner or later. Ask yourself... go ahead and ask,

"What matters? Do I matter? Can I matter? Does mother Teresa matter?"

Are we all clay, molded into one shape or another just so we can

differentiate amongst each other?

Are we like the letters of the alphabet?

Just different by shape but all letters at the end?

Letters have their own purpose. To make up the words through which

I convey our ability to not matter to the greater. Die I say. Or live I

say. There is no need to wear a mask or hold a smile for those around

you. You wear the mask for yourself. You chisel into stone or draw onto

the beaches' sand right or wrong for yourself. You're doing all this for

someone whose purpose is unknown. Yourself.

Then life is a cycle because we end up right where we started...

...pure sweet beautiful nothingness.

"How do you help someone

who doesn't want to be helped?"

A SILK BLINDFOLD

A curtain pulled over a population's eyes,

A burden not needed yet for it they cry,

It's not that those masses are unaware,

Of the harmony present or the love that they share,

It's that a preference of ignorance seems to prevail,

A passionate lot, yet to thier demons they hail,

An educator's voice drowned by this self-imprisonment,

All aspirations lie fried on an electric fence,

A comfort with discomfort,

An acceptance of the unacceptable

A fear of losing love,

When love is the only thing untouchable,

A constant denouncement regardless of pleasure unfamiliar,

Heads shying away from thoughts breathing only of failure.

A question many have posed, never once gotten an answer,

Where has all the love gone now?

Why is it only blame that is transferred?

Why isn't one's sorrow and suffering,

The responsibility of the own?

Why is it that no matter how hard we try,

The solution is always blood and bone?

Why won't we take two-seconds to burn this silk blindfold?

And breathe once the air of clarity ridding our eyes of this mould.

Something here of an actual tangibility in high value we would hold,

In order to make cups for water one day we would need to melt gold.

But if complain one must to bring about love and trust,

Then end this us now wasted, drowning,

Deep and dead in false, created lust.

Just sitting, waiting, anticipating the day,

We become one with the dust,

Watching the sun go down with blinded eyes,

Away from beauty they must rust.

An end not visible yet for it they wait,

Where pride is a good enough excuse to berate,

A burden not needed yet for it they cry,

This silk blindfold around a population's eyes.

CHASING SHADOWS

Diving deeper and deeper within for answers,

Conquering the infinity outside,

A chase that could easily lead to a painful,

And undeserving demise,

But if one must take it upon himself to unearth the cause of our cries,

Fate self written: with death he may fall but as a legend he shall rise,

A life spent chasing beauty to share,

With those who have lacked its sweet taste,

For all oceans calm, all thunders quiet,

When love shares its momentary embrace,

Answers spilt and painted on walls by the greats of our kind,

Ever falling on deaf ears, unfortunate,

Life-having no pause or rewind,

Beyond the moment so perfect so whole,

When present for a second is a noteworthy presence,

Simply attaching ourselves to their words, we forever dilute

The entirety, their essence,

We make idols, chants, memorials,

Drowning in manufactured devotion,

Falling to our knees, begging to the sky, losing ourselves in emotion,

Because our personal greats are who we want to and must be,

And not being fulfilled means there is some lack, indeed.

Let the confusion roll as massive insecurity breeds,

For desire and hate have both planted sinful seeds

In all this self-chatter, we've lost the ability to listen,

To each other, to our hearts and souls, to the several that have risen,

And continue to spread what you and I know in our hearts to be true,

Lack is only in thought; all else is perfection, complete and ripe for you,

Look and listen for the truth within

And then at this beautiful world just waiting around.

Reality, mere illusion, must be owned to completion

Then not one shall stand in your path or make a sound!

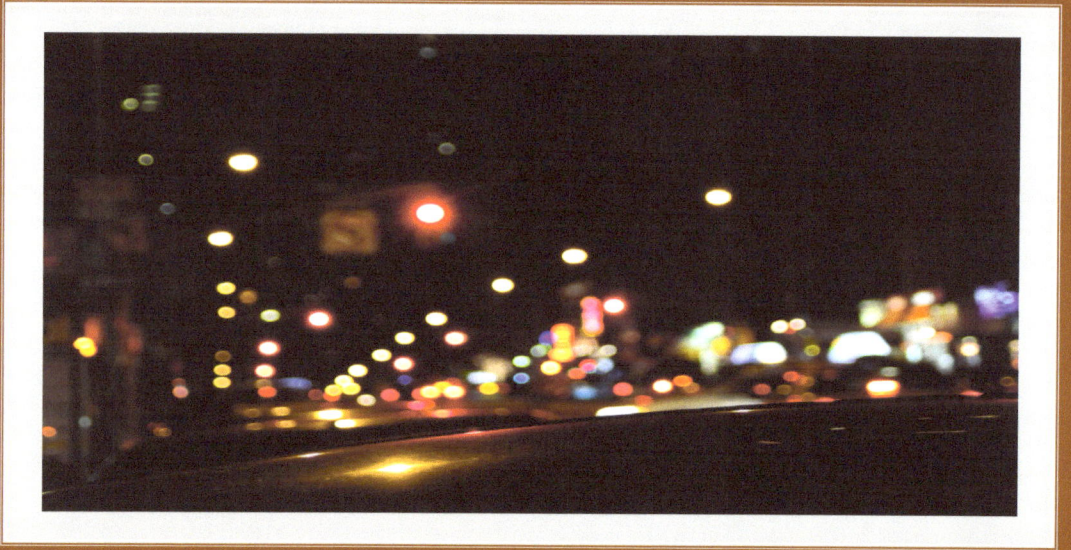

"Evil Must Exist for Good to fulfill its Duty. Every Yin Needs a Yang and Every Night a Day. The balance of life"

HERE I LIE BROKEN-I AM GUILT

❧

I am the first-born child of your conscience,

I flow through your veins, the step before penance,

I chain you to the likes of sanity,

I chain you from the sin you are to bleed,

You are strong, he who breaks away from the chains of their conscience,

The devil on your left shoulder has turned the other one into ash.

Either it is your heart or your mind that screeches through your soul

beyond all measure.

Else I would be able to stop you.

My voice is now replaced by another's.

Like a drug that blinds you from reality,

By melting us into its hallucinations.

The new voice leashes your neck and says only one thing,

"Burn the world into a pebble of coal."

I'm tired and weak of trying to hold you back.

You're drive to wrong, overpowers my mode of attack.

One day I know that you will overstep me,

But I vow not to budge for as long as I breathe.

You see no one in the distance. The iron is hot, figuratively of course.

Then why is your vision blurred? Why do your palms melt into sweat?

Why are you ready yet not at the same time?

How could you possibly have doubts now?

After perfectly contemplating the proceedings moment by moment,

What stops you now? Me?

Think. Vengeance is a curtain and from the naked eye it is only the

blood seeker without the drapes that alter your vision into believing

that what you are doing is somehow justified in the order of the

universe. Like you wrote it.

Your vision is indeed blurred by the liquid tears formed by the glands

tickled by me using your partially resurrected conscience as a medium

through which to attempt to slap some form of sense back into you.

Your vision is blurred because I want you to see the consequences that you will endure before you lift your hand to do the good deed. You are a human being!!... I tell you in Morse code...and you ignore me.

Trust someone did, that with your life, some good you will do.

Now you see down its throat and its teeth, hell now embraces you.

Not the hell that Satan rules, and not the hell that swallows heavens rejects,

The hell that you created for yourself, the hell that allows no self respect.

The key is not living forever as the pirates say,

But living with yourself forever, as dark as night will be day,

You killed. You raped.

You destroyed and harmed.

You took from him everything. You made them cry.

Wash your shirt, wash your hands, yet the stains of sin will never rid your soul.

The hell that you feared, of which you now are in command, population you.

In the mirror do you see the horns, the teeth, the devilish red skin?

Or do you see the family of the victim or have you gone blind?

Are you melting, proving only to yourself that you are indeed human?

With each hack you hacked off a span of your life.

The entropy of hatred has hence risen by your choice.

Sure you got away, but you can't run fast enough from me creeping

behind you.

You stepped through the door now fall through this black hole.

I've lost you, now don't ever come back,

Or I shall finish you!

Life doesn't deal a hand it lets you choose.

You strive all your life but now to yourself you lose.

I tried to stop you but now to shreds you will tear.

From the inside out I will eat, of my power you weren't yet aware,

Guilty conscience, guilty consciousness, will eat you alive,

Eat yourself human, before I feed you your painful demise!

"The cruel reality of others can sometimes jolt us into

appreciation for our own good fortune."

JUST ANOTHER

I came home joyous to my family after an exhausting day of labor,

As I entered my home I lent a smile to my neighbor,

And again I smiled when I saw God in the eyes of my family.

My life that moment was perfect; today it all seems a vanished dream.

As my wife brought me clear life in a glass to rid me of my thirst,

I see my children bicker over who can sit in my lap and share with me first.

Then I heard a loud thunder that shattered the pure village silence.

The screams got louder, nearer and our fear rose immense.

I ran outside to make sure all was right,

And since that moment I haven't shaken the sight.

Young devils, blood, flesh and chaos spread everywhere,

Children and women being dragged on the floor, at gunpoint by their hair.

These red-eyed young demons dressed in blue,

Looked like they had escaped from elementary school.

Allied with lies to enforce pride's Militant rule,

Killing our young male futures and our girls they would use.

Yet they marched to our house and pulled us all out,

Shoved a gun in my face and covered my youngest child's screaming mouth.

Knocked me down to the ground and as they started tearing my children

away.

My wife screamed in vain but…gun shot! Dead, her body now lay.

Fighting the tears, blood and shock burning on my face,

I was shivering as I felt life leaving her last embrace.

She took her children's names right before she died.

I lied motionless long after my voice left and my eyes had dried.

I look up now asking, "Is there really a god left,

"Whose eyes can see all but his heart is at rest?

"Elsewhere people can sit their entire lives and not feel true loss,

And here where we value life with evil our paths must eventually cross."

I ask, "Where is the fairness in this hypocrisy?

"Now where are the healthy and powerful democracies?

"Stuffing beyond measure while we are losing the young and hungry,

"But it has always been and so it shall be,

"Those with nothing must for another's excess bleed."

"Change is inevitable. It is for us to decide which direction we will steer the next chapter of our journey."

OVERCOME

Constriction is what his soul's neck has been accustomed to,

Shackled to his demons and insecurities and the reason is you?

You sliced his wings and latched an anchor to his feet

And told this bird to fly, watching, as he landed on his teeth,

He's tasted blood from you more than salt,

No candy canes, no chocolate malt,

No pat on the back, no sports games, movie theaters, no friends,

No unconditional love and only in his dreams would he get to see
the Grand Canyon,

"How is a burden on this earth ever to stand onto his feet?"

You made a child ask himself that,

Never was he taught to the stars one can reach,

The psychosomatic developed due to a spineless child's fear,

Praying to hear a heartbeat audible and clear,

For an unbiased embrace to hold me tight hold me near,

One cannot see the heavens around him no matter how hard he tries,

If he is brought up in darkness

Because someone keeps throwing mud in his eyes,

But once that shell breaks take a breath you better run,

The contrast of darkness taught him where to taste light,

Your reign, your dwindling power, your lack of...your done!

Wait, quivering for that one day, sit tight,

Now he has learned to Overcome...

Demons all slain and obstacles destroyed,

He has now learned to conquer Fright.

THE CHAIN BEGINS WITH WHO AM I?

Am I man or animal?

Animal or spirit?

Spirit or Energy?

Energy or Strength?

Strength or Force?

Force or Change?

Change or Rebellion?

Rebellion or Reaction?

Reaction or Action?

Action or Evolution?

Evolution or Insanity?

Insanity or Chaos?

Chaos or Revolution?

Revolution or Resolution?

Resolution or Resolve?

Resolve or Determination?

Determination or Strength?

Strength or Energy?

Energy or Spirit?

Spirit or Animal?

Animal or Man?

Man or all??

So say I is a man

I think therefore I am?

I know that I can

But what exactly is that can

And if that can is removed from the man is that man now cannot?

And if man cannot then can that I be?

I is then by definition can

And cannot by that same definition becomes nothing.

Existence of the I itself is the execution of the action then.

That which we call Purpose; that fills our every moment,

Existence of I is purposeful in the moment then.

No matter what that man "thinks" of himself,

Then let I am be what I is. At this moment words…

At the next, only the present presence of that I is what knows.

I am…

"Weakness is simply the fear stopping one from doing what they know in their heart to be their existence's purpose while depriving the world of their beautiful unique voice"

CHANGE-THE TRUE ARMS OF CONFLICT

A spectacle of a war is coming, due now just any day,

Clouds darken, the sky, rain, hail and thunders rage,

Armies preparing arsenals for what they know is yet to come,

The Earth can quench its thirst once again in foolishness' blood,

But man's self imposed anger must manifest one way or another,

Else we would be running in circles wondering why we have mothers,

We would start asking bigger questions,

And then start jumping off cliffs,

For we have not one answer to anything that matters,

Yet we are stiff,

Stubborn adamant all knowing creatures,

With the keys to our own bliss,

Forgive my French, but the greatest presences know:

They know not shit,

We want to know is all we really know in our narrow understandings frame,

But we talk!

We open our foul mouths to display our hate, our arrogance,

And the bystanders gawk!

And we eat up the attention like pudding holding our chests to the sky,

If any one man knew anything relevant tell me once,

Why would we ever feel the need to cry?

When we see beauty or feel pain,

Or why would we ever feel the need to lie?

Why would people continue looking up,

To those who only share empty pride?

When all we need to do is take,

About an honest fifteen-minute look inside,

The lack the soreness the depression we see,

Is not present in the world today,

It's in our thoughts; it is within us, in the fears that lead us astray,

Fight we must every second, with every inch of our being,

But keep in mind the first enemy is not what we are seeing,

Conquer the darkness within once and for all with love and forgiveness,

And you will conquer and become for eternity that which is endless!

"I wasn't aware of weather it was time or me that were standing stillness then, but all I know is that my eyes had captured the definition of perfection in that single moment when I had seen you that first time"

ONLY HER...

Your Eyes could tame the perfect storm,

How are you real for even roses have thorns?

Just a gentle touch of yours and I can breathe again,

Turned even a disbeliever with a smile that moves this pen,

To say what my lips couldn't dare to say,

I want you in my arms two days before yesterday,

You are who I've been looking for,

Since Infinity and beyond allure,

If I could put it in words a random jumble at best,

"You make me feel a funny tingle inside my chest?"

Best not to contaminate purity with the illusion of words,

So just be mine and mine alone and let the world observe!

WORDS...

If I could I would bow down to thee...

With you I could befriend the worst enemy...

Encompassing underneath your vast magnitude...

Is our race: humanity's historicity ...

Without you even a whisper left incomplete...

That is the power of life's most glorious subtlety...

Such a wound has never been inflicted ...

Such a light has never been spread...

Not a single thought shared between lovers...

Romeo never felt the beauty Juliet had said...

Never once think that I have taken you for granted...

It is with you, never for you, that every prayer is chanted...

So for now please accept this simple form of gratitude...

For this world, this book, this page would be empty without you!

"Follow Only Your Curiosity in this Journey of Life

for Questions Can Never Be Wrong"

May the feeling of fulfillment exist within you, within every single moment of your existence. Right now, and no matter what, triumph in every walk of life by sharing this enormous sense of joy you possess with those in the world around you in need of it. Let this be your cycle of life counting blessings instead of shortcomings.

Thanking You With All My Heart

-Rishi Jaiswal